**MAJOR LEAGUE
BASEBALL
PLAYERS GUIDES**

How to Play the Infield

Sandy Alomar
Matty Alou
Luis Aparicio
Glen Beckert
Ken Boswell
Leo Cardenas
Bill Freehan
Bill Mazeroski
Don Mincher
Thurmon Munson
Joe Pepitone
Brooks Robinson
Manny Sanguillen
Ron Santo
Joe Torre

GROSSET & DUNLAP   A NATIONAL GENERAL COMPANY
Publishers   New York

The illustrations are from *Make the Team in Baseball,* copyright
© 1960, 1966 by Grosset & Dunlap, Inc. Reproduced by permission
of the publisher.

All rights reserved
Library of Congress Catalog Card Number: 72-183014
ISBN: 0-448-01166-2 (Trade Edition)
ISBN: 0-448-06442-1 (Library Edition)
Published simultaneously in Canada
Printed in the United States of America

Contents

How to
Play
the Infield

Playing the Infield

MOST GROUND BALLS that get by a fielder go *under* his glove. So an infielder must concern himself first of all with playing close to the ground. Too many players just do not like to bend low enough. They either bend their knees and try to keep their backs straight, or they bend their backs and try to field with straight legs.

To field ground balls successfully and consistently you have to bend both knees and back. Note the stance of a big league infielder, especially a third baseman who may expect a bunt. He will be crouched so low that his chest is not much more than the length of his forearm off the ground.

But you must not only crouch low, you must get your glove down too, or you will not be able to smother

7

Your head should be right over the ball as you field it.

ground balls as you should. A good infielder plays right in the dirt and often brings up a handful of infield dirt along with the ball.

Of course to field a ball, you must keep your eye right on it until you have it in your glove. That means that your head has got to be right over the ball as you field it, with your face down toward the ball—not twisted away to keep from getting hit, or turned toward the base where you hope to throw the ball. You cannot be ball-shy in the infield. Bend right over and watch that ball until you have it safe in your hands.

The proper fielding position is in natural stride posi-

8

If it is a hard hit ball, you may have to drop to one knee.

tion, with one foot forward and your glove out in front of your forward foot. Of course, if there is an unexpected bounce, you may have to make a sudden adjustment. If you have your eye on the ball, your hands will make that adjustment automatically. Or if there is a really hard hit drive—and this happens most often at third base—you may have to drop to one knee and get your hands and body all in front of the ball just to block it and keep it in front of you. And slow bunts too require a special technique. But the normal ground ball is fielded in stride position with the hands out front.

Throws are always made overhand when possible.

9

The split second you lose by straightening up to throw overhand is more than made up for by the extra power and accuracy of the throw. Underhand and sidearm throws will dip and curve and give extra problems to the baseman. You use them only in instances of extreme urgency. But you still throw fast. You come up out of your fielding position *throwing,* ball in your bare hand, arm cocked, and looking immediately for the target. You cannot afford to reach back or wind up like an outfielder. Sometimes you may have to make a quick hop to get your left foot forward in throwing position. And you must always look right at your target as you throw.

A good infielder must have range. That is, he must be able to move quickly either right or left to reach a ground ball, and he must charge every ball that comes straight at him. He must also be ready to turn his back to the diamond and scamper back to get under a pop fly. But the lateral movement is the crucial one. A great fielder is not the man who avoids errors. He is the man who can accept the most chances—that is, get his glove on the most ground balls. Naturally, there will be many he will not be able to make a putout on. But he will also field many that a lesser man would not even reach.

To field and throw well, hands, arms and legs must all be in good shape and well warmed up. As you get into your crouch to watch for the ball off the bat (and you must look for *every* ball to come to you) make sure your arms and wrists are supple and loose. Flex your wrists, even shake them a bit to rid them of any stiffness. And make sure you do not crouch with your elbows inside your knees. You must keep your arms outside your knees, or you may have to take half a second to unlock yourself before starting after a ball.

A sidearm throw is sometimes necessary, but only when there is no time for the overhand throw.

And to get a good start after a ground ball, you must have your weight forward, on the balls of your feet. Your stance does not need to be exaggerated, although some infielders do like to go into a low, low crouch as they await the pitch. But you can have your back bent and your weight forward. And your arms should be away from your body. If you like you can crouch with hands on knees, and move them off with the pitch.

Then *watch* the ball. Some fielders watch it all the way to the plate. Some watch the plate and pick up a view of the ball as it comes in. Either way, you must look for the ball to come straight back to you. Every ballplayer needs desire, but the infielder needs it more than most. He must actually *want* that ball to come straight at him.

The balls that come straight at you are the hardest to field. It is somewhat harder to judge the hop and the speed of the ball when it is coming right at you. But these are the ones to practice on. Practice charging right in on them to smother them in both hands out in front. After you have had a lot of practice you will learn how to move in so as to nail the ball on the short hop, adjusting the speed of your approach so you get your hands on it at the right moment. But first of all you must just concern yourself with getting to the ball fast.

On balls hit to your right or left, you must move to get in front of them. But do not back off to round them up. Cut straight across the path of the ball to reach it by the shortest route and try as hard as you can to get your body in front of it. You may even have to make a big hop off both feet to come in front of the ball. Of course there will be balls that you will just have to stab for with your glove. But when you do that you must realize that, if you miss, the ball is going through to the outfield. On balls hit to your barehand side you must make a special effort to get in front of the ball. A backhand stab at a ball has a good chance of missing it and letting it go through for an extra base. But if you get in front of the ball you will at least block it, even if you cannot field it cleanly.

Now and then, you will find that ground balls will come streaking by that you just have time to dive for. But do not ever get into that position unless it really is a desperation play and you *really* have a chance for the ball. Don't do it to show how hard you are trying, because you are no good to your club when you are lying on the ground.

12

While we urge you always to *come up throwing,* we do not mean you should ever throw blindly. You should look to see if the baseman is at the base. If he is not, take a few quick steps in his direction while you wait for him. And don't throw to any base unless there is a man there to take the throw.

Infielders have to catch fly balls too. Generally an infield fly is a pop that is easy to catch. Just remember to catch it at good height so if it does bounce out of your glove, you will have another stab at it before it strikes the ground. The only really difficult fly balls will be the ones hit over your head, that you must go back for. You cannot play these as an outfielder would, running back with eye on the ball. And the worst way to try for them is to back-pedal after them. What you must do is pick out the spot where the ball will likely drop and then turn and scramble to that spot, then look up to spot the ball. It is possible to glove a ball like this with your back to the plate if you have confidence. You may find that you have to reach out a little farther than you would think, for the ball will probably be curving away from you slightly. But stay with it. Tell yourself you *can* catch the ball, and you will make the out.

The sun will sometimes bother you, but you should not give up to it any more than an outfielder does. If there is a bright sun that will give you trouble, you may want to wear sunglasses on your visor. (Be sure you can flip them down quickly. Practice this!) Or you can use your glove to shut off direct glare and judge where the ball will fall, then try to spot it when it comes out of the sun. Just don't quit on it. At least stick your glove up and *try* for it.

Also you may sometimes have to chase foul balls toward the stands. Know where the stands are and where the dugout is. And bear in mind that the ball will be likely to spin *away* from the stands if it is coming down close, so stay with it until you are sure it is a lost cause.

As you desire every ground ball to come your way, you must want to catch every fly. Whenever you see one you have a chance for, go after it and stay after it until someone calls you off. The pitcher usually captains the infield on short pop flies, and he will yell who is to catch the ball. If you chase a fly into the outfield be sure to yell for it. And remember too that the outfielders may be too far away to hear you at once, so keep waving other players away as you go after the ball. There is no excuse for colliding with another fielder. Sound off loud and clear. Signal with both arms. And listen to what the other guy is yelling.

All infielders have to take throws from the outfield on certain plays to relay them to the plate, or to other bases where runners can be headed off. The shortstop and second-baseman do most of the relaying. But every infielder must be practiced at it. The general rule here is to let the outfielder throw long and you throw short. As soon as the ball is hit to the outfield, you tear out on the grass in a hurry. You should go as far as your judgment tells you you should, depending on the depth where the ball is recovered and the strength of the fielder's arm. (It is up to you to *know* about that.) Then take your stance where he will make a long throw to you and you will make a relatively short throw to home plate or elsewhere. To make sure he spots you, keep your arms waving above your head. But do not turn so you lose sight of the runner, or runners. You do not want to have to look all over the diamond for the runners before you throw. So keep the runner in the corner of your eye as you await the throw.

You want to take the throw high enough so you can

14

Take the fly ball high, so you can get off your throw immediately.

get a throw off quickly. If the ball starts sinking as it approaches, then run to meet it. If it comes in too high, back off enough to take it about at the height of your shoulders. By the time you have the ball, you will know where you want to throw it. All the same, look to see if there is a play. Perhaps the runner is faster than you thought and there is no hope of catching him. Or he

15

may not represent the winning or tying run and it may be better to nail a careless runner at second or third, to choke off a rally, in preference to chancing a tight play at the plate. Here again you use your judgment. Others may tell you where to throw. But *you* must decide if you have a play there. If you throw blindly where there is no one to take the throw, or no runner to tag out, that is *your* fault.

When an outfielder is throwing to the plate, one infielder acts as cut-off man. Your manager will have special cut-off plays, with specific men to handle the ball. But if no one gets in position to cut off the throw to the plate, then *you* do it. You should always be looking to get into *every* play.

The cut-off man awaits the throw part way down the baseline, where he can keep track of what is happening on the bases. He is no good if he is out on the grass where he cannot see the runners. For he must cut off the throw or let it go, depending on whether there is a chance for an out at home or not. If the throw is too late to get the man going home, then it must be cut off. But once you have decided to cut it off, you do not need to wait for it. Run to meet the throw. The sooner you get it, the sooner you can make the play. Again be sure before you throw that there is a baseman to take the throw and a play to be made.

If no play can be made, hold on to the ball! Do not just throw a ball automatically to a base. That goes for fielding a ground ball too. If the runner has the base made, keep the ball. A throw always means an additional chance for an error. Do not make them when there is no use.

Get in the habit too of backing up every throw. When one man goes out on the grass to act as relay man, then another fielder should back him up, about thirty feet

16

(half the pitching distance) behind him. Don't wait for the other guy to do that. It's *your* job unless there is someone there before you.

Good ballplayers always back up throws, when runners are on the lines, even the throw from the catcher to the pitcher, because sometimes that can get by and trickle on into center field.

The First Baseman

THE ONLY place for a left-hander to play in the infield is at first base. At any other position he will be at a disadvantage on most throws. A right-hander can play first too (some of the best have been right-handed). But if you are a lefty and want to play the infield, this is your spot.

As you practice for this position, you must always work with a base, or some imitation of a base. You must get used to working around a base, and always be conscious of where you are in relation to the base. Your big job at first base is getting to the bag to take a throw and you have to develop a sixth sense for the location of that bag, so you never have to flail around wildly looking for it.

Your very first move, on every batted ball, unless you are actually involved in fielding it, is to get to the bag. Run for that bag fast. Maybe the runner is slow and the

Ready position.   *Waiting for the throw.*

play is easy. But you be on the bag ahead of time. Move! Don't ever keep the fielder waiting. Sometimes even a short line drive over your head can develop into an out at first. So don't stand watching it while you "concede" first base. Get to the bag and be ready!

Of course you do not take your position right on the bag. You stand on the inside of the bag—the second base side—and face the ball. You should have one foot

Stretching toward the throw.

either on the bag or within inches of it. Glance down at once and make sure just where the bag is in relation to your feet. There are few things more pathetic than the sight of a first baseman with the ball in his hand vainly stabbing with one foot for a bag that is not there.

Tell yourself that every throw is going to be a bad one, then you will never be taken by surprise. Stand with your knees bent, holding your glove up for a target,

19

When it's a choice between
getting the ball and leaving
the base, leave the base.

and ready to move in any direction, to stretch to the ball, to dig it out of the dirt, or to take a throw over your head. But give the fielder a target.

Don't get yourself into a stretch position before the ball is thrown. It may be a wild throw and you will have a hard time recovering and getting after it.

As we said, look for a bad throw. If it is coming on target, and the play is close, then get your foot on the base (right foot if you are right-handed, left foot if you are left-handed) and *stre-e-etch* toward the ball. The point of stretching is to save a tiny split second on the runner. But do not tag the base with your heel. Use your foot. If you use your heel the stretch will pull you right out of contact with the base. At the same time, take care not to plant your foot in the middle of the base or you'll be nursing a fat spike wound. Give the runner his half of the base.

If the throw goes into the dirt you will have to field it as if it were a ground ball. Get down to it! Bent knees. Bent back. Head down over the ball. Watch it right into the glove.

If the throw is high you do not necessarily have to leap for it. With a quick hop you can get back into foul territory with your toe on the base, and may be able to take the throw without losing contact with the base.

Of course when it becomes a choice between getting the ball and leaving the base, you leave the base. Better stop the ball from going through, *first*. Sometimes you can even scramble back and make the out.

All first basemen agree that the toughest throw to take is the one that goes "right into the runner." A throw to the home plate side must sometimes be plucked right off the runner's chest, and you have to remain cool and confident to handle this one. You stretch out toward the runner but keep your glove in fair territory, in front

21

of the runner, and you may have to make the catch while almost touching the runner with your glove. But he has no right to run into you or interfere, so you need just to keep your cool and try to make the play as if he was not even there.

If the throw is wild on the home plate side and pulls you down the baseline, you can often make a quick tag on the runner by just letting your glove swing right on after you get the ball. Stay cool and confident and you will make many an out on the home plate side of the bag.

When a ground ball or pop fly is hit down your way, you have to leave the covering of the bag to somebody else and go after the ball. Don't hesitate to range to your right freely after ground balls. Cover all the ground you can on that side, as long as you feel you have a good chance for the ball. Don't play the wooden Indian and stand and watch ground balls hop through the hole while you tell yourself the second baseman will get them. Anything you can reach on that side is yours.

You do not often have as good a shot at a short out-field fly as the second baseman or the right fielder may have, because you will probably have to turn your back on the ball. But go after such balls until you are called off, and if you know you can catch the ball, yell for it and wave the other players off.

On ground balls you field to the right or behind the bag, the pitcher becomes the baseman and it is your job to get the ball to him to enable him to make the putout. Remember this, however: It is always better to avoid a throw if you can. If you make the play close to the bag and you *know* you can beat the runner there, wave the pitcher off and go make the putout yourself. A throw always means an extra chance for an error. And if you can save your pitcher a few steps, that's all

It is sometimes necessary to take a bad throw from in back of the bag.

to the good. He has plenty of work to do at his regular job.

When you make your throw to the pitcher covering, try to time it so it will get to him in the most comfortable manner (for him). Try to have it reach him before he gets it to the bag, so he does not have to be looking for the ball and the bag at the same time. It should come to him about chest high—a straight soft underhand toss. One thing you want to take extra care about when you make this throw is not to hide the ball

23

from the pitcher. Sometimes you see young fellows try-ing to give the play an extra flourish by snapping the ball from under the glove. That is the wrong way to do it. You must pull that glove right out of there so the pitcher can see the ball as you hold it in your hand preparatory to throwing it. Then give it a swift easy toss right to him, so he can take it two or three steps his side of the bag.

A bunt down the first baseline is usually a play you have all to yourself. If it is not too close to the line, the pitcher may be able to get it easily. But if he misses it, the ball is yours. And if it goes to your left, it is all yours anyway. You have to move in fast on a bunted ball. And when you anticipate a bunt, or when the batter squares around in bunting position, you charge right in toward the plate at top speed, body low, ready to field the ball out in front of your feet.

Some young players concern themselves too much on this play with the danger that the batter may sud-denly haul off and rap the ball hard or chop it over their heads. That is something you should not give a thought to. Charge right in fast, looking for the bunt. If you are alert, determined, and confident, you will react swiftly to any shift by the batter. Play the bunt and other plays will take care of themselves.

Once you have fielded the bunt you have a choice of going to knock off the lead runner or making the obvious out at first. Before the play even develops you should have considered all the possibilities. A throw to third? A throw to second? You know you are going to have to pick the ball up fast, within a stride or two, to have a play at either of those bases, because the runners will be starting off a good lead. Suppose you do get the ball in your hands quickly. Now you *look* at the base to be sure you have a play. Perhaps the runner, having cheated on the pitch, is already there. Maybe the third baseman charged in and nobody covered. Maybe there is no one covering second. In a fraction of a second you have to note these things yourself and decide if you can make the out. There will be people yelling to you to throw to second or to third. But don't throw blindly. Look first and be sure. Then make your throw hard and fast.

But if you see there is no play, never mind what anyone is yelling. Turn and make your throw to first, *inside* the baseline. The runner has to stay to the right of the baseline on this play. Don't hit him in the back. Once in a while, if the ball is bunted hard and retrieved at once, this can be a tag play, for the runner will be coming right past you and you can flip him with the glove as he goes by.

Your other big job at first is holding the baserunner on. There will be times, depending on the score and the style and ability of the batter, when your manager will want you to forget the runner and take your regular position behind the baseline and toward second base.

Most of the time, with a runner on first, you will be holding. The spot to play then is on the outside corner of the bag. Be careful not to stand with your feet blocking the runner. It is against the rules for you to block the baseline when you are not holding the ball.

Watch the pitcher. Hold your glove up for a target. And be ready! Above all, be sure you are familiar with the "move" the pitcher has on this play. Some left-handers especially have really deceptive moves. While a pitcher usually keeps his striding foot low to the ground when he pitches from the stretch, so there will not be so much time for the runner to get a start on him, some left-handers like to lift the striding foot fairly high and this often fools the runner into thinking the

25

On the pickoff play, stand on the outside corner of the bag.

pitcher is committed to the pitch. But don't let it fool you! You stay right on the bag, with that glove up until you *know* he is going to the plate with the pitch.

When you take the throw from the pitcher, swing your glove down to the right to put the tag on the runner. Get the ball right down between the runner and the bag, turning as you do to see where he is. If you turn to the left, the way some old-time right-handed players used to do to add style to their play, you may find the runner has evaporated! He may already be on his way to second base and will have a good start on you.

You will probably have a pick-off play worked out with your pitcher in certain situations to take the runner off guard. On this play, you will apparently give up on the runner and go back to your normal fielding position, then dash in quickly and take a snap throw from the pitcher. And your catcher too may be snapping throws to you in a hurry sometimes when he sees the runner is

26

too far off the bag or is "leaning" the wrong way. The catcher will also be throwing to you on a dropped third strike or even on an attempted double play when there has been a force at the plate. Throws like this should come to you in foul territory, for the catcher will be well behind the plate and you can give him a better target on the foul side of first.

Many managers judge the skill of a first baseman by his ability to make the double play by way of second base. In throwing to second, a left-hander has a decided advantage for he cocks his arm with the normal swing of his body. A right-hander, however, after fielding a ball on the first base line or near it, has to twist his body in an unnatural direction in order to get off a throw. You will find if you are right-handed and have to throw from the foul line to second base that you will do better to follow the natural swing of the body all the way around to the left. Then you will be throwing more naturally, with more body in the throw. Again the time lost will be made up for by the speed of the throw.

In making the double play from the second base side of the bag, a right-hander can often just plant his feet and throw with a quick swivel of the hips from left to right to get the body into throwing position. This takes a little practice. You will observe that as you swing the hips, the left knee will bend almost to the ground before you can get your whole back into the throw. And you may still find it easier, if the throw is a long one, to make the complete turn around. Whatever you do, remember the play is not complete until you get back to first and take the return throw. This means you have to *scramble*, get back to the inside corner of the bag, foot on the bag, glove held up for a target, and stretch toward the throw as soon as you see it coming.

It used to be that coaches would always urge first

basemen to "Take every throw with two hands if possible." No longer. Since introduction of the big trapper mitt some years ago, it has become far more natural to use one hand on all catches, even pop flies. It is the "normal" way to use the big glove, with the bare hand brought in only to cover bunts or any ball where you must come up throwing. Then you have got to use both hands, for you want to get the ball into your throwing hand as soon as possible. But first you want to be sure you *have* the ball, so you stay down close to the ground, with your eye right on the ball. A bunt often may be rounded up with the glove and grabbed in the bare hand. Just remember you cannot throw it until *after* you have taken a secure hold of the ball.

There is a lot more to playing first base than anyone can set forth in a book. The job at first base is what you make of it. You can hold the job with your bat if you want, limiting your range to about the spread of a turkish towel and contenting yourself with just catching the good throws. But if you do that, you had better have the best bat in the league, for you can hurt your club badly here. The best first basemen learn to range up the baseline toward second, to take off after all pop flies, fair or foul, within reasonable reach, to charge the plate on every bunt situation and to make the other fielders look good by getting right down to dig out bad throws as if they were bull's eyes.

There is always more to learn about the job, about the leads that different runners take, about the speed of certain bunters, about the habits of your other fielders in throws or coverage. You often act as cut-off man and must learn to keep one eye on the runner as you await the throw. You can help your pitcher and catcher by offering big targets on pick-off throws. And you can make your pitcher's life easier by making unassisted

28

putouts on ground balls near the line. You should work and work at your job until you can find first base in the dark. And you should learn to stretch until you get the last possible inch, to nip those speed boys at first. The first baseman who catches with his arm short, that is elbow bent and legs not fully stretched, may turn a good pitcher into a loser. But the man who can reach w-a-a-a-y out there to get the throws a half step sooner can help turn a mediocre pitcher into a winner.

The Second Baseman

MOST OF the physical contact on a baseball diamond takes place around second base. No man who is the least bit queasy about contact should try to play second base or shortstop, for once the enemy learns that you don't like to mix it, you will get a steady diet of body blocks and high spikes and take-out slides. This does not mean that you are going to get into a roughhouse every day. Once you make it clear that you will hold your ground and make your putouts against any opposition, you will find that the other guys begin to respect your courage and try to stay clear of you, to avoid the putout.

A powerful arm is not a number-one requirement at second. Of course every infielder has to throw hard and long on occasion, as on relays. But at second most of the throws are short. Getting rid of the ball quickly and hitting the target are the important qualifications. A second baseman must also be ready to charge a slow ground ball fast and throw across his body accurately without taking time to stand up, plant his feet, and face his target.

Like every infielder, a second baseman should practice around his base continually—and should practice hard. He should work especially hard on the double play with the shortstop, taking his turn in the pivot and learning how to get off the throw to first in the least possible time.

The strategy at second base is always affected by the strength and the style of the batter, as well as the tactical situation. A left-handed pull hitter allows the second baseman to close up the hole toward first.

The batter's speed will indicate about how far away from the bag the baseman can play, for if you are looking for the double play you cannot get so far away as to give the batter the four-plus seconds usually needed to get to first. A right-handed pull hitter allows the second baseman to cheat toward second base, for he must cover the base if the ball is fielded in the shortstop position or at third. If fielders are properly stationed —not too far behind the baseline or too far off the base —the double play can usually be completed in under four seconds, and that is enough to beat the man coming down from the plate.

But the second baseman must be wary of the place hitter, the man who is looking to bounce a hit through whatever hole is left open in the infield. With that sort of hitter at bat, the second baseman cannot afford to move too far toward first base to close the hole, or he will leave a wide gap over second. So to play this position properly, you must know the habits of the batters you face.

30

When putting the tag on, turn the back of your wrist toward the runner.

It will pay you, therefore, if you are not familiar with the club you are facing, to study the other side's batting habits during their batting practice.

A second baseman must learn how to tag a sliding runner, for many of the runners hit the dirt on coming to second. You put the tag on by holding the ball in *both* hands and getting it right down between the runner and the base, where the runner must slide into it. When you do this, be sure to turn the *back* of your wrist toward the runner. The inner side of the wrist has more tender skin and there is a regular network of small blood vessels there, so you can very easily collect cuts from spikes—cuts that you would avoid by turning your hand around.

You have to get your head right over the play when you put on the tag. Do not just stick your hand down and lift your head and hope. The runner may deliberately slide past the bag and reach out to touch it with

31

If you hold the ball down too soon . . .

his hand after he has gone by. Wait for him with the ball in both hands, your feet straddling the bag, and your knees bent. Then, as he slides in, bend right down and put the ball where he has to hit it. Hold your ground, no matter how fierce his slide. Putting him out will more than repay him for any bump he gives you.

If he does slide past the bag to avoid the tag, be sure to keep the ball between the runner and the bag. Don't leave the bag to chase after him. He has *got* to tag the bag. If the ball is between him and the bag, you can lay it on him as soon as he tries.

Don't make the mistake of holding the ball down too

. . . the runner has a chance to kick it out of your hands.

soon, expecting the runner to slide peacefully into it. If he sees the ball there, he may decide to kick it out of your glove as he comes in. Have it ready, then shove it down between his leg and the base as he comes in.

On balls hit to the (batter's) right of second base, you will sometimes have to make a throw to second. It will be an awkward throw, because you will not be in normal throwing position as you field the ball and will have to twist your body to the right to get any force in the throw. Probably the easiest way to do that is to hop off both feet and land with your left foot forward, facing the base. But many good second baseman like to swivel the hips with the feet planted, dipping the left knee as they turn the body to the right. This gives them all the power they require to make that short throw, and make it with force.

Slow hit balls must be charged by the second baseman, because the runner may be moving faster than the ball and you have got to get hold of the ball and snap it to first before he gets there. Drag bunts that get by the pitcher may have to be fielded by the second baseman, who has to come right in on the grass after them. When you field a ball that is rolling to a stop on the grass, requiring you to snatch it up in your bare hand and sling it to first in almost the same motion, you should not use the regular technique of getting your whole body in front of the ball as you approach it. Instead you must run by the ball, to the first base side, and pluck it off the grass as you go. But be sure you keep your eye on the ball every second, until you have it in your hand. Resist the temptation to look at the base or the runner. Take hold of the ball first. This is one of the easiest balls to miss, if you take your eye off it for even a moment. In charging ground balls of any sort, do not try to get hold of them at the halfway point of the bounce. Just move right in and smother the ball out in front of you. If you try to adjust yourself to get hold of the ball at the "right" height, you will find the ball is playing you, when you ought to be playing the ball.

When the first baseman is pulled in to field a bunt, it is up to the second baseman to get over and cover the bag. When you are taking a throw from the first baseman or pitcher or catcher from inside the diamond, behind the runner, give the target for the throw *inside* the baseline. And leave the runner his share of the bag. Get your own toe on the bag *before* the throw comes.

The second baseman is sometimes better positioned

to field short flies into right field or pop fouls behind first base than either the first baseman or the right fielder is. At any rate, if you are playing second base you should go after such flies unless you are called off.

A second baseman should always remind himself of the speed of the batter. If the ball is hit to the second baseman's position, the race is often neck and neck. If the man at bat has extra good speed, then you should edge in a little closer to the baseline and stay crouched and alert, ready to charge the ball the instant it leaves the bat.

Of course a second baseman is always judged, as a shortstop is, on his ability to make the double play. In getting two for one, the second baseman may be either the fielder or the pivot man and he must know both jobs perfectly. When there is a man on first base with less than two out, the double play is always a possibility and the second baseman moves in a few steps closer to the baseline to shorten the distance to the bag and thus speed up the play. If the batter is right-handed and known to pull, then the second baseman can move still closer to the bag so he can reach it in a tearing hurry.

When the second baseman fields the ball in a double play he must deliver it to the shortstop covering the bag in such a way that the shortstop can move smoothly to make the out and be able to get the throw off to first with no lost motion. That means that the ball should come to the shortstop at throwing height, near the shoulders. And he should receive the ball *before* he reaches the bag. He does not need to be fumbling after the ball and trying to look for the bag all at the same time. You cannot therefore fling the ball recklessly toward the bag. You must time the throw or toss properly. You must be facing the target. And you must deliver the ball high enough so it can be thrown quickly.

When you field the ball close to the bag, you can use an underhand toss to feed it to the shortshop as he comes to the bag. Just be sure however that the shortstop can *see* the ball. Do not hide it behind your glove. Face the shortstop, pull your glove out of the way, and give him a good fast toss about chest high, timed to reach him when he is two or three steps on the other side of the bag.

When you are a good distance from the bag, toward first base, you will have to throw the ball. Do not be timid or hesitant about the throw, or try to "steer" it to the shortstop. Pick up your target and use a straight hard overhand throw. Of course you will be trying, as always, to get the ball to him before he reaches the bag, and to deliver it at throwing height.

Do not, however, be *too* eager to get two out on a ground ball. If the runner has got a good jump, as on the hit and run play, and you cannot make the out at second, go for the sure out. Do not try frantic off-balance throws when the runner has the base made. Better one out than none. And better one out than an overthrow that lands the runner on third.

When the ball is hit on the shortstop side of the bag, with a runner on first and less than two out, you become the pivot man in the double play. You job is to get to the bag fast, so the shortstop will not have to hold the ball waiting for your approach. And of course you have got to be there ahead of the runner. If the man on first base is a real speedster, you had better cheat toward the bag just a little to make sure you can get there in plenty of time.

The throw will come to you, ideally, as you approach the bag. But do not start reaching out for it before the shortstop lets it go. You have to expect every throw to be off target, and be ready to adjust to get in front of it.

36

If the throw is to one side or the other, hop over to get your body in line with the throw, so there will be no danger of its going on into the outfield.

You cannot throw the ball of course until you have got it in your hand. But you must also tag the bag for the force-out before you relay the ball on to first base. To do that quickest, you step right across the bag, to the infield side, and tag the bag with your trailing foot. Then you face first base squarely and let go a hard overhand throw, inside the baseline, to the man at first to nail the hitter.

It is very important that you remember to square around and face first base before you get your throw off. Otherwise you are likely to miss the target and to throw with only about half the necessary speed. Turn your body right toward first, pointing your left toe at the target and step right out as you fire the ball.

It is a serious mistake to try to stay on the base or astride the base on this play. The runner will be coming right for you and his aim will be to take you right out of the play, to make it impossible for you to throw. If you keep going across the base, he will still go for you, but you will be on the move and can jump right clear of his slide.

Once in a great while, when the throw is late and the runner is right on top of you, it may be good tactics to remain on the outfield side of the base, to push back from the base as you tag it and make your throw outside the baseline. But don't get in the habit of playing it safe on the double play just to avoid any risk of contact. You have got to establish your right to the area around the base.

Don't be chicken about fielding a ball on the baseline either. The defensive man has a right to make his play and it is up to the runner to avoid you if you are making

When the throw is late, push back from the base as you make the force . . .

a legitimate effort to field the ball. If he runs into you when you are fielding a ball, he is out.

Second base is an action station and it requires a player with a lot of heart and real desire. It is part of the crucial defensive "middle" that determines the strength of a ball club. If you play that position you have got to *want* to get into every play and be ready to put a tag on

. . . and make your throw outside the baseline.

any man whenever it is required. You must make up
your mind nothing is going to go through, and must be
ready to charge full tilt in on the grass, leap as high as
you can after line drives, or run all the way to the foul
line after pop flies. You will also frequently be covering
the base on a steal and you must get in there astride the
base to wait for the throw and get right down close to

tag the runner. If the throw from the catcher comes in low, do not leave the bag to make your catch easier. Hold your position and dig that ball out of the dirt. Cutting down these steals can give a real lift to your pitcher and make his job easier all through the game.

The Shortstop

THE SHORTSTOP is the key to the defense. Often he is the team captain. And whether he is or not, he is generally the "holler guy" in the infield, the man the club depends on to keep the defense on its toes, to relay the pitching sign to the outfield, to decide and signal who will cover on an attempted steal. He is the man usually involved in the pick-off play at second. He covers third base often on a bunt down the third base line. He acts as relay man on most throws from center or left-center field. He has to "go back" often for short fly balls and chase pop flies to the third baseline and beyond. He fields everything he can reach, from the balls hit over the pitcher's mound, to those that may get by the third baseman.

Obviously he needs a strong arm, for he often has to fire the ball from deep in the hole near third base or relay it home from the outfield. He should be in the habit of making his throws overhand, with lots of power. A fielder who steers the ball instead of gunning it is not going to make good at shortstop.

While not all shortstops have been speedsters, a man

40

has to be agile at this position and have wide range. He should be able to cover the whole width of his position rapidly, get rid of the ball in a hurry, and maintain his balance at all times.

Most ground balls are hit through the shortstop's position and many of them come through with a lot of sizzle, particularly if they bounce off artificial turf. A shortstop therefore must play his position fairly deep, so he has time to get the range on ground balls and not let them handcuff him before he can move.

But the exact spot in which you play will be affected by the habits of the batter, the manner in which the pitcher is working, and the tactical situation. A right-handed pull hitter permits you to close up the hole toward third. A left-handed pull hitter lets you move closer to second base. But if the man at bat is a spray hitter, you cannot play him to hit too far right or left. He will be looking for the hole and trying to hit through it, so you must not make it too wide. Likewise, when your pitcher is working outside to a right-handed batter, you do not need to concede him too much ground on your left. Outside pitches to a left-handed hitter mean you must not open too much hole on your right.

With a runner on third base in a tight ball game, you will very often be playing to cut off the run. This means that you will be in closer to home plate to shorten the throw. And it means you have to be doubly alert to react if the ball is hit your way. There is no time, in this position, to think about the hop. You get your hands on the ball as fast as you can and come up throwing—that is, ready to throw to the plate. If the man on third does not break for home, however, you must get the ball fast to first. Sometimes you can bluff him back with a fake throw, then fire to first.

While you will always make overhand throws when

possible, there will be times at shortstop when you have to take desperate measures to beat the runner: sidearm throws, underhand throws, quick slings in almost the same motion that you pick up the ball. It would be a good idea therefore to practice all these throws. You will observe that the overhand throws fly straighter and bounce truer. But when you have no choice, you should be able to get the hurried throws on target too. Just be sure there *is* a target—a man covering the base—and that you look at him and move toward him as you throw.

A shortstop charges every ground ball. There will be rare ones that will be on top of you before you can move and on these you may have to fall back a step to get your hands on the ball. But you should plan to charge every ball and tell yourself that every ball is coming to you. Slow hit balls especially need to be charged hard, to shorten the throw and beat the runner.

The third baseman will be trying to cut off many of the balls hit to your right, for if he can field them in close, he will have an easier throw. But sometimes, on difficult balls that pull him a long way out of position, you will be in a better position to throw. In those instances, don't hesitate to tell him so. Yell that you have got the ball and yell loud!

When a runner is likely to steal, it is up to the shortstop to exchange a signal with the second baseman to tell who will cover the base. A simple signal is best—a movement of hand or glove to indicate either "You take it" or "I'll take it". If you are going to cover (as you probably will when there is a left-handed pull hitter at the plate) you must break for the bag as soon as the pitcher lets the ball go to the plate. You will be at the base, straddling the bag and waiting for the throw by the time the catcher is ready to fire it down. Hold your ground against the runner and put the tag on him with

42

You should be at the base, straddling the bag and await-ing the throw.

both hands—with the back of your gloved hand toward the runner.

Of course there is sometimes a double steal called, with runners on first and third. Most clubs have a signal agreed on to indicate what the coverage is to be when a double steal seems likely. You will have to use the signal to indicate to the catcher that you will cut off his throw and fire it right back to him to get the man trying to score. On this play you must charge right in toward the mound and cut off the throw on the grass, then rifle it back to the plate.

But if the double steal is not anticipated, and you are going to cover second base against the steal with men on first and third, you still have to keep half an eye on that runner on third. It is best for the second baseman to cover in this situation because he can keep the runner in view more easily and then be ready to slam the ball back to the catcher if the man on third does break for home.

Any time a sign is given be sure *both* guys know what is planned. In other words you must have some signal for the other guy to give that indicates he has understood the sign.

There is of course no way of telling for sure just what a runner is going to do. But you should always try to figure out the possibilities. With a three and two count on the batter and a man on first, there is always a good chance the man will be running, so you should prepare for him. Is he fast? Does he often try to steal? Is the batter a good hit-and-run man? Figure these things out and you will know if you should play a little closer to the bag and break for it when the ball goes by the batter. If you have a good bat-handler at the plate who likes to hit and run, and if he is ahead of the pitcher, then you must take care not to offer him too much of a hole to punch the ball through.

The shortstop is the man who almost always works the pick-off play with the pitcher, to trap a runner off second base. Nobody can afford to stick to the base to hold the runner on, and it is not necessary to do that anyway, because a pitcher is allowed to fake a throw to second and he can bluff a man back whenever he wants to. Also the shortstop, playing almost behind the runner, or the second baseman, whom the runner usually keeps one eye on, can fake returns to the base and keep the runner leaning back toward second.

The catcher often gives the sign for the pick-off because he can see when the runner has got himself farther away from the base than the shortstop is. But you can give it too, and you must practice this play with your pitcher, because it is done on a count and you must

44

both be counting at the same rhythm if the play is going to work. Once the sign is given, the pitcher "forgets" the runner, turns to face the plate and starts to count. The shortstop starts to count too, and on the agreed count he breaks for the bag and the pitcher turns and throws the ball to him. If the runner has got himself farther away from the bag than the shortstop, he is almost a certain out on this play, because he just cannot start soon enough to beat you there.

Shortstop and second baseman must practice together constantly to become familiar with each other's moves on the double play. When the shortstop throws to the second baseman on this play, he must try to get the throw chest-high to the man. You always throw to the man and not to the bag. And you should deliver the ball to him before he reaches the base. If the ball is tossed, the glove should be pulled out of the way so the baseman can see the ball all the time. You should move toward the base as you throw and get it to him fast so you will not keep him hanging in the pivot too long. The second baseman does not see the runner on this play as he waits for the throw, and he needs to get his hands on that ball before he gets to the base, so he will be able to concentrate on making the out and avoiding the runner.

When you, as shortstop, play pivot on this play, you have several advantages. You will have the runner in view as you approach the plate, and you will be facing the right direction for a throw to first. You must take care however not to over-run the base so as to get the throw *after* you have crossed it. If the second baseman is slow in getting the ball to you, you can shorten your steps quickly so as not to hit the base too soon. You want the ball with you when you get there. You make your tag by stepping across the base to the outfield side and dragging one toe across the base. Just be sure you get that toe on the bag before you jump clear. You come in to the base rather low, with knees bent, so you can have spring enough to get speed into your throw. As you throw, you of course face the target.

Whenever you throw to first base, you should make it a habit to step toward the target. This makes your throws more accurate, provides more power, and takes a lot of strain off your arm.

Arms and legs and hands—these are what an infielder depends on for his bread and butter. Keep them in shape by working them out all year round. Don't let hands get soft or wrists get stiff or legs begin to gather lard. Run and run in your off time and do plenty of throwing—*after* you have warmed up. You can practice fielding anywhere at any time—even without a ball. Just keep charging imaginary ground balls and grabbing them out in front, with knees bent, back bent, and head down over the play.

The Third Baseman

THIRD BASE is named the hot corner because balls come down there hard and fast and because a lot of crucial plays are made there to cut off scores. The third baseman often has to deal with balls that get to him too fast for him to charge and he must be ready to go right to the ground, on one knee, in front of such blows to block them, even if he cannot always get them in his glove. He tries in fielding such balls to close up all the openings, as a catcher does when a pitch is in the dirt, with legs or feet together, and glove closing the gap.

But the third baseman must be ready to field normal ground balls too, by charging and fielding them in his natural stride. He has to get rid of the ball faster than other infielders do because he has a longer distance to throw the ball. A third baseman needs a strong arm, of course. Some third basemen have become pitchers because they could put so much smoke on the ball. But more than strength they need quickness, an ability to snatch a ball out of the dirt or off the grass, to cock the arm quickly and let it fly without taking time to recover balance or wind up.

The third baseman fields a great many bunts and slow rollers. He has to develop judgment in the handling of these balls and he has to be conscious at all times of just where the other baserunners are and what sort of jump they may have got on the pitch. That requires intense concentration and alertness, as well as the sort of split vision a basketball player uses to keep track of where his teammates are.

There are batters who make a habit of dumping a ball down the third baseline any time they find the third baseman either playing too far behind the baseline or "playing on his heels"—that is, standing up straight or nearly straight, and relaxing. You just can't relax at third base as long as the ball is in play. You must keep your eye right on the ball, keep your weight forward at all times, your arms and hands away from your body, your knees well bent, and your back bent too, to be as close to the ball as possible if it comes toward you. And, like every infielder, you keep telling yourself that *now* it is going to be hit to you.

If a bunted ball rolls down along the baseline, it is often good strategy to wait for it to go foul, which it often does if it is right on the line. Then, when it is in foul territory, brush it away from the diamond quickly with your glove. Such balls have been known to roll fair again if a fielder leaves them alone. But if the ball comes toward you on the grass, you are going to have to pick it up and get it over to first. You cannot take these balls head on. You just approach them to one side, actually running past them to the left, so you can pluck them up in the right hand and fire them off without straightening up. There is a very real danger on this play that you may look at first base too soon, for of course you must look at your target before letting the ball go. But if you lift your eyes from the ball before you have it firmly in your hand, you may very well leave it lying there on the grass, with nobody near it and the runners romping along the baselines.

The third baseman of course does not field every bunt. Some do not come up the line far enough and can be handled by the catcher. Some that are halfway between mound and baseline can be cut off easily by the pitcher, particularly if he anticipates a bunt. When there is a runner on second base, it is important that you work out with your pitcher the details of how you will play a bunt. If the pitcher can get to it, then you should scamper right back to the bag to be ready to make an out there, killing off the lead runner.

To make a force out at third, you need to just get the ball in your glove with your foot in contact with the bag. So you act like a first baseman, reaching out toward the throw and making sure your toe stays on the bag. You have to remain awake, however, to the possibility of turning this into a double play. Making the out at third leaves the force still on at second and at first. If there was a runner on first base and he did not get too quick a jump, you may be able to fire the ball down to second at once and nail him. But *look* to be sure the base is covered and that you do have a play.

If there was no runner on first, or if the runner has got off to a fast jump and has the base made, there is still a chance for the out at first, for the batter naturally would not take off until after he had bunted the ball. Always look for that extra out on this play.

If the play at third base is a tag play, then you should take the throw while straddling the baseline edge of the base. Make the tag with two hands if at all possible, turning the back of your glove to the runner and getting the ball right down between him and the base. Get your head down too, right over the play, and do not let the runner scare you out of there. Wait for the throw, knees bent and glove out to give a target. If the throw is low, hold your position and dig it out. If it is a little wide, reach for it. Always expect it to be off target and do not reach until the ball is on the way, or you may not be able to adjust to a bad throw. Only if the throw is off target do you leave the base and go after it.

The third baseman ordinarily plays just a stride or two behind the baseline. He cannot afford to get too far back, although a left-handed hitter may permit him to move a good distance toward the shortstop position to close up the hole. From this position you go after every ball on your left that you think you can reach. You poach on the shortstop just as often as you can, unless he calls you off the ball. Because you are playing closer to the plate than he is, you can often field a ground ball before he can, and will be able to save a little time on the runner.

With a runner on third base, you play a little closer to the bag, although you may move away from it before the pitch. While not too many runners will try to steal home, you may still be able to trap one who takes too generous a lead. Usually he will watch you and move as far away from the base as you are. If you want to try a pick-off you may have a sign with your pitcher, indicating you will break for the bag as soon as the pitcher, in pitching position, looks at the plate.

And because many runners will break hard for the plate with the pitch, you should break for the bag as soon as a pitched ball goes by the batter, giving your catcher a chance to snap the ball down to you to trap the runner.

A runner on third with less than two out will of course be looking to score after a fly caught in the outfield. You cannot do anything to keep him from trying, but you can make sure he does not take off *before* the ball touches the outfielder's glove. When such a play is developing you should stand in foul territory where you have a full view of both runner and umpire and remind the umpire loudly to watch the runner. Keep pointing at the runner and keep your eye on him. If he does take off too soon, you must make your beef right away. Don't wait until the runner is called safe at home, because then the umpire will not take you seriously. But if you get your protest in before a play is made on the runner, you may persuade the umpire that you are right. Or you may help wipe out any doubts in the umpire's own mind as to whether the runner got started ahead of time.

In the later innings in a close ball game, you will need to play a good deal nearer to the bag, to shut off the possibility of a batter's rifling a ball between you and the base. Those baseline hits spell extra bases, and you cannot afford to let them get by in a close game. Even if you cannot field a ball, if you knock it down and keep it in front of you you can keep it from doing real damage to the home cause.

Your exact positioning on the diamond will be affected, just as is the positioning of any other infielder, by the game situation and the way the pitcher is working. Tight pitches to a right-handed batter mean more chance of shots down the baseline. Outside pitches allow you to move more to your left. Curve balls and change-up pitches give the right-handed batter more chance to pull the ball and when one of those is coming, you should be prepared to break to your right. You can work out a sign with the shortstop (who can read the catcher's signals) so he can tip you off to the pitch.

Often on a short fly to the outfield, on which there is no real chance to score, a baserunner will nevertheless make a good strong bluff toward the plate. On this sort of fly you use different tactics from your play on a regular sacrifice. Instead of moving out into foul territory, you move well down the line toward home, inside the diamond. You can still watch the runner to see if he takes off ahead of time. The shortstop will cover the base while you are down the line. Then if the runner does try or pretends to try for home, you are in the right spot to cut off the outfielder's throw and bang it back to third base, or hang the runner up in a rundown.

Most plays around third develop fast and must be handled with great urgency. But you have an advantage in being closer to the plate than the "middle" fielders. A hard-hit ball will reach you so quickly that you will usually have all the time you need to knock it down, then pick it up and beat the runner at first. Pop flies into fair territory behind you will ordinarily belong to the shortstop, because he can get a better line on them. But don't give up on them until you know somebody is after them. And go after fouls between third and home. You are better equipped than the catcher to handle these. If the catcher has a better shot, the pitcher will call it.

The third baseman usually has to decide where the throw should go when a long fly is caught in deep left field with runners at first and third base, and less than two out. He should *know* right away if the runner on first is tagging up or going halfway down the line. If he is tagging up, he is going to try to advance. Then, if the throw is coming in too late to catch the man trying to score, the third baseman should cut it off and try for the man going down to second.

The third baseman has got to be thinking and moving all the time, and must have good peripheral vision, or eyes in the back of his head. He has got to keep track of what the runners are doing, to determine if he has a force out at third or if there is a better chance to make an out at some other base. When he lets the pitcher or catcher field a bunt, he has got to get back to cover the base and still *know* where the throw is coming from. He should also know a lot about the speed and skills of the base runners, so he can tell whether a man has got such a good jump that there is no use making a play on him.

For some reason there have been, in baseball history, relatively few really tall third basemen. But there never has been such a thing as a successful third baseman who didn't have a lot of courage. To be ready to move in fast on a slow-hit ball or get down and block a hard-hit ball, or even give a step or two to a ball that rockets to the ground right in front of you, or leap for a ball on the way up over your head, to stand up to a baserunner and put the tag on him without flinching, to move in a step or two on a batter who is aiming to whack the ball right "down your throat"—that takes guts, agility. and strong, strong desire.

A Word for All Infielders

As a matter of fact no man can play the infield without strong desire—desire to get into *every* play, to back up *every* throw, to cover *any* unguarded base, to field *every* ground ball, to catch *every* pop fly, to throw out the fastest runner alive. In this part of the diamond, you are likely to be in the midst of explosive physical action at any time. So you must know what is going on and what is likely to happen—what the score is, what the skills of the batter and runners are, what the pitcher is trying to do, how many outs there are, what base is open, where the force plays are, what sign the catcher has given to the pitcher. You must be ready to trap any unwary runner and hustle to give your catcher a target on any pitch that goes by the batter with men on base.

It may be that an outfielder can afford a glance at the score board or look over to see what is causing the ruckus in the stands. But in the infield, your attention must be absolutely undivided. And you must be ready to get right down in the infield dirt to dig out ground balls and make tags. Every effort you make has got to be a total one, or you not only will not come out on top in the game, you will never derive from the game the rich satisfaction it can provide to a guy who goes into it with all his heart and soul.

Remember that tag plays are made at the *front* side of the base, so you bend into a tag play. You do not back away from it.

Nobody can set out for you all the many situations that may develop on the diamond. You can learn how

As an infielder, you are in the midst of the most explosive action on the field.

to handle them only by being right their and experiencing them. There is *always* something to learn about infield play, so there is no such thing as too much infield practice.

When you practice, do not fool around. Get into it with *game* spirit. Talk it up! Run fast! Throw hard! Encourage your mates! Applaud good plays! Keep moving! Keep thinking!

By getting into hundreds of different situations and fielding thousands of ground balls, you develop your reflexes so you will react automatically and with lightning speed to whatever comes up on the diamond.

Never shy away from a rough play. Show the other

guy that you are not afraid to get hands and body and head right into the fray. If your muscles are strong and well-conditioned, your body in top shape, and your reflexes sharp, you are not going to get injured. But if there is an ounce of chicken in you the enemy will exploit it.

Move fast into and out of your position, glad to get your chance at bat, eager to get back into the action.

Never look for an easy way to make an out. Take the direct way, no matter how much contact it seems to promise.

There is no such thing as too much running and throwing either. If you take care to warm up before every practice—even before batting practice—you are not going to do yourself any harm by practicing hard at throwing and running, practicing until the perspiration pours off you and soaks your shirt. Throwing and running may make you feel tired eventually but they will improve your wind, strengthen your arm and shoulder, and increase your muscle tone, so that you will experience that wonderful sense of well-being, of enjoying every second of being alive that only a well-conditioned body knows.

The Catcher

DON'T LET anyone tell you that a catcher can be a big dumb slob who doesn't feel pain. A catcher nowadays has to be smart, quick, and aggressive. He holds the job that probably requires the most courage, the most brains, the most baseball savvy, and the best physique. There may have been times when catchers could be big, fat and slow, but that time is not now. A catcher's reactions have to be fast, to scramble after bunts and foul pops, block bad pitches, and get off quick throws to any base. With the whole game in front of him, he has to be the chief strategist on a lot of plays too, acting as "captain" on bunt plays and cut-offs, and making sure the fielders are positioned so as to take advantage of the kind of stuff his pitcher is throwing. He has to keep baserunners from stealing and make put-outs at the plate.

The catcher has to know the hitters or, if he does not know them, be able to figure out from stance, swing, or general behavior at the plate, what the batter's weakness and strength may be. He has to be alert for giveaway changes in stance or batting grip. And he has to keep his pitcher in a confident, aggressive mood.

So the catcher's job is a big one. No wonder so many catchers have become big-league managers—from Branch Rickey to Ralph Houk. A catcher is always learning and always has his eye on the ball. A fellow who loves to play and to study the game and who enjoys taking charge is the sort of player who is likely to make a good catcher. He may be husky or lean or extra tall or just average in height—as long as he is smart, quick, full of confidence, and able to inspire confidence in his mates. Often a catcher sets the whole tone for a team by getting them off in a fighting, winning frame of mind by his own aggressive way and by the manner in which he keeps the club on its toes.

Nowadays a really small fellow has a hard time making it as a catcher. Managers (and pitchers) like big fellows behind the plate. Rangy guys, who can reach 'way out to block pitches, are a comfort to the pitcher.

But a guy of average size, as long as he reacts quickly and is not afraid to get his body in front of the ball, can usually make up in alertness what he may lack in height and reach. Still, a small, light fellow is better off at some other job.

The catcher's important qualities are knowledge of baseball and eagerness to get into every play. He can yell to the fielder what base to throw to, can advise the cut-off man whether to stop a throw or let it go through, can warn his fielders to be on the alert for a bunt. But to do these things he has to know his way around a baseball diamond better than most men and he has to have confidence in his own judgment. If you decide to become a catcher, therefore, you are not only applying for the biggest job in baseball, but for the most demanding and—if you really love the game—the best.

The catcher needs strong hands, a strong arm, and strong legs. He must be able to grab and hold a hard-thrown ball in a tight, unshakable grip. He has to throw the ball hard, too, and throw it accurately. While he does not put the strength into *all* his throws that a pitcher does, he still throws the ball as often as the pitcher and he frequently must throw it farther, with great speed and accuracy. And his legs must be strong to permit him to crouch at every pitch, and to leap quickly out of his crouch and move in any direction.

What this means is that you have to exercise hands, legs, and throwing arm continually to keep them strong and supple. Your throwing arm must be kept in shape with as much care as a pitcher uses. You should *always* warm up your throwing arm before using it full strength. Take fifteen or more easy throws before you get into a game and begin to fire the ball hard. And make it a habit in all your practice throwing to throw at a target and to take a step *toward* the target as you throw. The catcher cannot afford to wind up when he throws, and he cannot reach back the way a pitcher does before letting the ball go. Often he must unleash a throw from right behind his ear, without even coming fully out of his crouch. But if you take care in practice to step as you throw and to throw overhand, with the full length of your arm, your arm muscles will develop properly.

A good tight grip is provided by strong forearm muscles. Clench your fingers and notice how the muscles of your forearm tense and harden. Here is where you must build muscle if you are to have the grip a catcher needs. Constant squeezing of a rubber ball provides a simple exercise that you can practice at all times and in all places. Rowing, hammering, digging, ropeclimbing, push-ups on the finger-tips—these are all exercises that will help build those muscles.

The best exercise for the legs of course is running. But a catcher must also keep his legs limber by deep-knee-bends and work of that sort. These exercises should not be done halfheartedly or spasmodically. A regular regime of running and walking, with knee-bends, should be followed. And running does not mean idle jogging or a couple of wind sprints in cool weather. It means real running until the breath comes short and the sweat pours. Exercise of this sort is not just a means of warming up. It is maximum effort to build strength and endurance. Even a pitcher does not always have the demands made on his endurance that a catcher has to face. Besides doing his job behind the plate every day, or nearly every day, a catcher is expected to contribute solid hitting and good baserunning to the cause and he must be an extra infielder on bunts, foul pops and throws to first base.

Equipment

Assuming you have the mental and physical qualifications, you must then give some thought to your equipment, particularly glove and shoes. Nowadays the catcher has a choice of glove styles and he will find expert performers who will argue in favor of each style. Some men insist on the break-rim glove that allows them to fold the glove right over on the ball and become a "one-handed" catcher. This keeps the meat hand out of the play until the ball has been safely gloved and it greatly lessens the danger of broken or jammed fingers. But the break-rim glove, according to some catchers, sometimes deprives the pitcher of strikes because the catcher, to take hold of some pitches, must slap down on them, knocking them out of the strike zone, catching them lower than need be, and influencing the umpire to call them below the strike zone.

The solid rim glove, according to those who favor it, helps the pitcher because it allows the catcher to take low pitches with a lifting motion, keeps low strikes in the strike zone and makes it easier for the umpire to see that they are strikes.

So there is a trade-off here—safe and sure catching with less danger of injury as against risking the meat hand for the sake of getting those low strikes. You should use the glove that provides you with the most confidence. If you are uneasy about your ability to grab and hold the pitches, you are going to transmit that uneasiness to your pitcher. So use the glove you feel sure of.

Shoes are of as great importance to a catcher as they are to a pitcher because the catcher often has to scurry out of his position to make a catch or receive a throw. Loose spikes or badly fitting shoes can cause him to

59

stumble and fall. Baseball shoes, because they are of light weight, have a lot of give to them and will soon stretch from use. It is a good idea, therefore, to get shoes that are a bit smaller than dress shoes. They will take some breaking in of course and this should be done gradually, to avoid raw spots and blisters. Sometimes a player is lucky enough to find a man with slightly smaller feet to break in his shoes for him. New shoes and new glove should be broken in during practice. A stiff glove can cause passed balls, so it is well to have two gloves and two pairs of shoes on hand—one breaking in and one for game use. Always inspect your spikes before putting on your shoes and do not go into a game with spikes that are working loose. They can betray you at a crucial moment.

Position and Stance

When you start actually catching pitches, it is good if you can work behind a plate of some sort so that you can get adjusted to its position. In a game you will work just as close to the plate as the batter's swing will allow you. If the batter stands deep in the box, you will have to allow him an extra few inches, so there will be no danger of your glove's interfering with his swing. If he stands forward in the box, you can move up too, because you want to make your throw to base just as short as you can. You will always catch in a crouch. But your crouch will be deeper when the bases are empty. Sometimes, with no one on base, and the pitcher in need of a low target, you may actually go to one knee. But you should *never* go that low with runners on, or you will be unable to get off a throw.

Choose the stance in which you feel most comfort-

60

Whatever your stance, always be ready to get off a throw.

able. There have been some catchers with legs so heavily muscled that they could not get into a really deep crouch. So work out the way that suits you best. You may find, as many catchers do, that you get better balance if you put one foot slightly in front of the other. You give your signs to the pitchers while you are right down on your haunches. With men on base you get your tail up somewhat higher and your knees only partly flexed. With the bases empty you can stay down until you receive the pitch. But you should form the habit of *always* taking the pitch so you can get a throw off without delay. As the ball settles in your glove, cover it with your bare hand and let both hands ride with the force of the pitch up to your shoulder. If you make this a habit, you will always be ready to get off a throw in a hurry.

You give your signs in a crouch, laying your fingers against your right thigh to indicate the pitch you want. Keep your glove out at your left knee so the third-base coach cannot see your sign. Keep the signs simple when the bases are empty, for no one will be reading them except the guys on your side. The standard signs are one finger for fast ball, two for breaking pitch, and so on. When you have men on base who can read the signs, you and your pitcher can agree on dummy signs. That is, you will give several signs and only you and the pitcher will know which sign is real. You can also have a take-off sign, or an agreement that at a certain sign the pitcher will throw the opposite of what is called for. High, low, tight, or outside, can be indicated by placement of hand on right or left leg or by motion of fingers and hands. And if you want to remind the pitcher, as you should, that there is a runner on first who may get frisky, just point a finger right at him. The pitcher too will have a brush-off sign and even a false brush-off, to help confuse or unsettle the hitter. Bear in mind that when there is disagreement between you and the pitcher, the pitcher must be convinced you are right.

62

Give your signs in a deep crouch.

Never insist on a pitcher's throwing a pitch he does not want to use. If necessary, go out and tell him why you want a certain pitch. And if he does not agree, then give him his way.

When there are runners on base, you must be ready to throw, to catch them stealing or prevent them from getting too big a lead. A catcher must always be ready

63

and eager to throw. There have been catchers who have been afraid to throw, for fear of making an error. Errors should not trouble you in practice. Always remember it is better to heave the ball right into center field, when you are practicing, than to aim it so carefully you cannot get it to the base in time. You achieve accuracy by throwing hard, with your eye on the target. Make it a constant habit always to throw to a target, and always to keep your eye on the target as you throw, and always to throw full strength.

Keep throwing until you *know* you can hit what you aim at. A catcher who is afraid to throw for fear of throwing wild is easy meat for base runners. It does not take them long to realize the catcher is hesitant about throwing. And once they know that, they will steal your back teeth. Let the baserunners know that you are always ready to throw to any base, at any time. When you do throw, come right out of your position, and step toward your target as you let fly. Do not be half-hearted about this. Explode right out of the chute like a Brahma bull and come out throwing.

Of course to be able to get your throw off quickly, you must get the ball quickly into your bare hand. Still, you have to take special care in catching not to extend your fingers toward the pitch, for a foul tip on the end of a straight finger can do real damage. So you must train yourself to keep your hand *folded*—not clenched—as you wait for the pitch. This is not as easy to manage as it may seem. If you watch catchers carefully, or look at pictures of them as they receive the pitch, you will discover that some of them, in spite of themselves, are sticking their fingers out straight at the moment the ball comes in. They are the guys who get the busted fingers and they may complain that they *always* keep their fingers folded and so can't understand how they

64

Let the baserunners know you are always ready to throw to any base.

get hurt. The fact is that they do not even realize they are not keeping their fingers flexed.

A good way to remind yourself to keep the fingers folded is to take hold of the rim of the glove as you await the pitch, then draw the bare hand away as the ball comes into the glove. Some keep the bare hand well away from the glove and bring it over to smother the ball *after* it hits the leather.

65

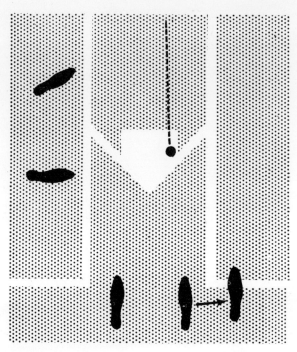

A good catcher always slides over to get his body in front of the ball.

But whatever you do, you must form that habit of bringing *both* hands with the ball back to throwing position after every pitch. Your glove, once you have given the sign to the pitcher, becomes the pitcher's target. Be careful to keep it up with the pocket toward the pitcher so he can get a good shot at it. If your feet are spread to give you good balance and the knees are flexed, your glove, held up before your body, provides a good big target with a bull's eye.

You must bear in mind always that your number-one job as you receive a pitch is to keep it from going through. So if the ball is well off target, you do not just stick out the glove on one side or the other. You slide your whole body over to get it in front of the pitch. This

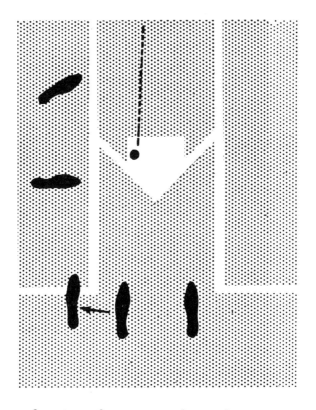

is always the sign of a man with catching instinct—he slides over to get in front of the pitch and does not try to be a first baseman or a trick-catch artist. He *slides*— as a boxer does or a basketball player. Do not use the crossover step. Make your first move with the foot nearest the ball. This will keep the width of your body always facing the pitcher and provide a wide obstacle. If the ball is in the dirt, the object is not to field the ball but to keep it in front of you. So you drop to your knees in the path of the ball and use your glove to close up any opening left by knees or thighs. When the ball is in front of you, the baserunner, unless he had planned to steal and is already on his way, is not going to have a chance to advance.

If the ball does get by, get after it! Scramble as fast as you can to get that ball in your throwing hand. Do not look at anything but the ball until you have the baseball tight in your fingers.

Another simple but important point is the proper positioning of the glove. If you are trying to catch a ball below the strike zone, turn the fingers of the glove down. Catching a low pitch on the heel of the glove invites a passed ball. Sometimes, if your pitcher is showing signs of becoming wild high, you may even want to get down and put the top of the glove right on the dirt in front of your knee to give him a good target. This sort of target is often a great help to a pitcher who is having trouble getting his curve ball down.

You must also take care not to become immobilized in your position. Remind yourself to move out from your spot every now and then. Walk out in front of the plate. Get out of your crouch and offer a word to an infielder. Make the whole plate area your own and feel free to move all around in any direction. If you stick in your crouch too long you may find it difficult to unlock yourself and move out to make a throw. Above all, do not get into a position with your elbows between your knees. That is sure to tie you up when you try to move.

Of course you have to start off with plenty of confidence—confidence that you can stand up to any pitch, confidence that you can get off a throw to any base, confidence that you are not going to get hurt. But to cultivate and inspire that confidence, you have to stay loose. So move around behind the plate and let everyone know you are there. Of course, you do not shift and twist and shy off when the pitcher is getting ready to pitch. Then you have to offer a steady target. Keep the ball always in your view. Don't let anything the batter may say or do bug you enough to turn your attention from your job. But between pitches, make yourself at home.

Working with the Pitcher

You and your pitcher have to know each other thoroughly, so you can communicate with as little hitch as possible. Naturally, if you are going to tell your pitcher what pitches to use, you have to know what pitches he can throw—and what he can control. That means, not just asking him what pitches he has, but finding out what he is doing best with *right now*.

Maybe the curve ball that was killing them a few days ago is not breaking today, or is hanging high. Maybe his fast ball has lost a little zip. Maybe he cannot control that hard slider. Maybe his change-up is working exceptionally well. Also he may have peculiarities you should be familiar with—a fast ball that breaks in a little, a screwball that has an especially sharp break. Be sure you know *all* the pitches a pitcher can throw and know what they look like when he throws them. Then find out how they are working *today* and be guided by that knowledge. Sometimes he may not even realize that something is wrong with a certain pitch and you may have to explain to him why you are not asking for it.

But don't let your pitcher—unless he is one of those once-in-a-lifetime guys—use the same pitch all the time. Even if, say, his curve ball is off the beam today, you must call for it now and then, as a waste pitch, so the batter cannot time the fast ball too easily. If the batter knows the curve is there and may show up at any time he is not going to be able to dig in against the fast ball quite so confidently. The main reason you *must* know

69

what pitch is working best today is that this is the pitch you must call for in a pinch. The general rule is *always* go with your best in a tight spot. Sometimes you may not be able to convince the pitcher of this right away. There are pitchers who have a habit of looking for some fancy pitch when they are in trouble. You have to talk them out of that.

As a matter of fact, a catcher uses a good deal of psychology in dealing with a pitcher, because he not only has to convince him that he is right about the pitch he wants, he has to keep him from losing his courage when things go bad—and from taking matters *too* easy when he has a good lead. While you never want to fight with your pitcher, there are times when you may have to stick in a needle. There are guys who have a habit of "tiring out" before they are really tired, or who begin to fight shy of the strike zone when the heavy part of the batting order comes up. And there are others who like to coast as soon as they get ahead. So you have to buck these guys up, encourage them or drive them as the situation seems to require, and make sure they are giving out with their best efforts.

You will find that all pitchers need to be told when they are going good—even the very best of them. And many of them have to be told they are going good even when they're not. No matter how sharp and strong your pitcher, don't forget to tell him about it. Yell to him. Go out and pat his back. Tell him how good he's looking. And if the batters start to get to him, tell him they're just lucky, that the next batter is going to pop one into the air, that he just needs to fire that good pitch in and they'll never straighten it out.

You should know your man well enough to realize when he is actually beginning to tire and to tell him what to do about it. Many times a pitcher without realiz-

70

ing it himself will unconsciously begin to ease up. He will pitch "straight up"—without getting his back completely into the pitch. He may shorten his stride, so his fast ball loses its fire. He may be leaning back a little too far and letting the ball go too soon, so that it is coming in high. He may be failing to "pull down" enough on his curve, releasing it too quickly as a result of taking too long a stride. Or he may be getting impatient, getting his body too far ahead of his arm, so that his pitches are missing despite the fact that he throws plenty of good stuff. Maybe he needs to move a shade to the right or left on the rubber to zero in properly on the plate. Perhaps he is aiming his pitches instead of firing them hard. It is up to you to help diagnose his trouble and tell him what to do. You can do that only if you are thoroughly familiar with his motion and his pitches.

Sometimes a pitcher may start to get disgusted with his own efforts and lose his concentration. Then you must help him out. Tell him what he is doing wrong. Remind him that there is only a short way to go, that you are all going to get him a lot of runs, that he has plenty of stuff left if he'll just bear down.

Or if he begins to get hot under the collar at a bum call by the umpire, or an error, or a lucky hit, it is your job to cool him off. Carry the ball back to him. *Make* him take a little extra time to get his composure back. Hold on to the ball an extra few seconds. Urge him to forget about what just happened. He'll get this next guy for sure! Maybe you can joke with him a little and remind him of how he has handled this batter in the past, or how well his curve has been working. All this is part of the catcher's job.

It is also part of your job to keep the whole club alert and to encourage infielders to forget their errors and concentrate on the *next* batter. Don't hesitate to take

71

charge, to give encouragement, to needle the guys who need waking up, to call for more zip and to try to pull the club together. And be sure at the same time that you are doing your *own* job with lots of aggressiveness and with fierce concentration. If a club begins to fall apart, with some guy sulking or putting on an act to show how disgusted he is with himself, or with some fielder doping off, it is the catcher's fault. He has everyone in front of him and it is up to him to set the example and call the tune.

As for your inning-to-inning strategy, this will depend of course on your knowledge of the hitters as well as the pitcher, and on the game situations, which we can discuss later. Just make sure you do know what your pitcher can do and try hard to stay ahead of the batter by observing his weaknesses and strengths and looking for the little moves and signs that may provide a tip-off to what he has in mind. Do not make the mistake of routinizing your calls, so that a batter can predict them. That is, do not set a definite pattern—such as high inside, low outside and so on. Keep switching your pattern so that the batter will not be able to outguess you. Sometimes you can give him two high tight pitches in a row and catch him looking for the outside pitch. A pitcher with good control can sometimes catch a baserunner flatfooted by throwing two waste pitches in a row. Of course that is giving a lot away to the batter but once in a great while it is worth it, especially if you have a pitcher who can throw strikes whenever he wants to.

The men who throw the ball hard are often the men who need the most handling. Many of them may show a tendency to go wild high and will start throwing balls to the backstop. You can help them with the good low target and by deliberately slowing the pace of their work—by keeping the ball in your hand a little longer than usual, by talking to them, by walking out of your position from time to time to shout encouragement, by making them wait a while for the sign.

The curve-ball pitchers also need that outside low target sometimes to keep the ball from "hanging." And you have to watch to make sure they are not striding too far on the curve ball but are giving themselves plenty of room to "pull down" on it.

Of course every pitcher will have his favorite "get him out" pitch. It may be a low screwball or a hard slider or, best of all, a good, hard fast ball. Generally speaking the low pitch is always best, because batters seldom hit low pitches for distance. But when a pitcher has a blazing fast ball that comes in across the letters, that is often the best medicine of all. A fast ball that really hums just does not give a batter a chance to time it and it is right on top of him before he can get a good look at it— so it always looks as it does at a distance, about as big as a Lifesaver.

Catching the Knuckleball

One pitch that can give any catcher trouble is the knuckleball. There probably isn't a catcher alive who enjoys handling those things. But if that is what your pitcher specializes in and he can get it into the strike zone, or near enough to it, you have to call for it to get the batter out. Over the years there have been all sorts of ways to catch this pitch and none of them works to perfection because nobody, not even the pitcher, can predict which way the ball is going to break. For a while, some managers thought they had licked the problem by giving the catcher a glove about the size of a manhole cover. But the leagues outlawed the extreme version of

73

this glove and the one allowed, while still much larger than the regular glove, did not prove of much help. It could not be folded over the ball quickly enough, being stiff and too wide for the catcher's hand to control. So there were just as many passed balls with the over-size glove as with the reguler one. And no catcher had time to get used to it, so it was awkward to handle and an annoyance when trying to catch pop fouls or take throws.

Ultimately, the catchers who seemed to handle the knuckleball best were the guys with the quick hands who could wait until the final second and then make a grab for the ball. Of course they had to have plenty of practice and even then pitches would get away. The point is, however, that the catcher has to call the pitch that the pitcher can do best with, and not the one the catcher can handle most easily.

Sizing Up the Batter

You develop a "book" on batters by seeing them often in action. But sometimes you have to size up a batter without any book and then you must depend on your observation of his stance and swing and the way he handles the bat. If you see a batter who likes to crowd the plate, so that inside pitches have to be in the strike zone, you can generally figure that he prefers to pull inside pitches. So you keep the ball away from him as much as possible and if you come in tight, you ask for the ball low enough so he cannot do any damage with it. The guys who stand away from the plate usually are the ones who like the outside pitch, or are not afraid of the pitcher's getting the ball out of their reach.

Sometimes, however, a batter will fight shy of the

plate simply because he is afraid of the ball and you can shake him up with tight pitches and crossfire. The batters who shorten up on the bat are usually the fellows who will hit the ball where it is pitched, and who are ready to go after anything in the strike zone, but are not so likely to blast one to the fence. These fellows take to the breaking balls least and are not so likely to do well with the high, hard one.

Bear in mind however that knowing the batter's strong point does not mean you sweat to stay away from that pitch at all costs. Naturally, you are not going to give him anything he finds easy to hit. But neither are you going to let him deny you the strike zone. You should be aggressive toward the batters and, unless there are good tactical reasons for pitching around a batter or for trying to keep him from bunting safely or for wasting a pitch, you should challenge them frequently.

A heavy hitter who comes to the plate in the late innings straining at the leash and obviously making ready to drive the ball into the seats can sometimes be suckered with a good fast ball right into the dirt. Again and again heavy hitters have swung hard at such pitches that start off looking good. Don't be afraid to call such a pitch on those very rare occasions when it may seem warranted. But don't forget one thing about it—the batter who swings and misses at such a pitch can *still try for first base,* even if you glove the ball. The rule says the third strike must be fairly caught and if you catch it on the bounce you are not catching it fairly. So stay awake on these pitches. Keep the ball in front of you at all costs and if you happen to glove it, put the tag on the batter.

Your job in general is of course to select pitches that will get the batter into a spot where he must take a cut

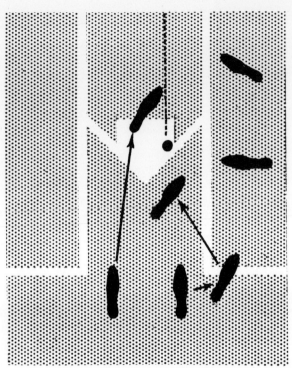

Getting out in front for a possible throw to first with left-handed batter.

at a ball he cannot do much damage with—that is, you set him up for the get-out pitch by putting him in a hole with other stuff. If you look on each batter as a special problem and figure out exactly what you can do to get him out, you are not so likely to get into a rut, or set a pattern the batters can begin to recognize.

Men on Base

The catcher's job becomes far more complicated when he has baserunners as well as a batter to deal with. Once you have a runner on, your strategy as well as

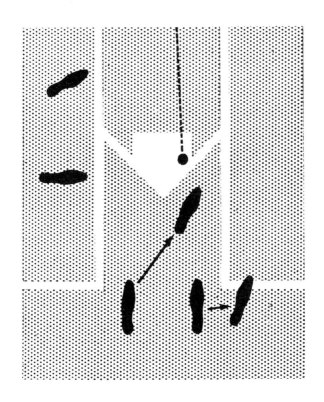

With right-handed batter.

your stance must change. You must consider the possibility that the batter may bunt, or may go for the hit and run, or that the runner may try to steal. You may have to call for a pitch-out to find out if there is a play on—to see if the batter moves into bunt position, or to anticipate the steal. And of course you must be ready to get off a throw, either to hold a dangerous runner close or to nail him if he tries for second. You cannot afford to get into a deep crouch. On every pitch you must make ready to get right out in front of the plate and let the ball fly. Or you must look quickly at first base after you receive the pitch, to see if you can catch the runner "leaning" toward second or taking too big a lead. (The runner usually moves a few steps down the line with the pitch, and if he does not get back instantly, you may be able to pick him off.)

If you throw to second to beat the runner, you should aim right for the base and get the ball in about knee high. This will put the ball right where the fielder needs to have it to make the tag easily. In throwing to first to catch the runner there, you throw on the *inside* of the bag about knee high, so the baseman has but a few inches to move the ball to put the tag on. Do not hesitate to throw down to first as many times as you need to, to keep the runner from getting too far off the base on the pitch. And make your throws hard and fast, without hesitation or attempts to "steer" the ball. Come right out of your position and use the ground you need to stride toward your target and fire the ball hard, in an overhand throw, without any wind-up.

With a runner on second, you may want to try a pick-off play, with the pitcher letting the ball go to the base without any preliminary look—just turning and throwing on a specified count that he has practiced with the shortstop. Usually you call this play (and you are the only one who can give the sign for it) when the runner gets farther away from the base than the shortstop is. It is sometimes called a "daylight" play because it is called when there is daylight between runner and short-stop. And of course when the runner on second base takes too long a lead, you must be ready to fire the ball down yourself, if not to catch him off base at least to shorten his lead and keep him "leaning" back toward second. Otherwise he may be able to score on a ground ball that would ordinarily advance him only one base. Bear in mind too that if the runner is allowed too much liberty off second, he can steal third, for he can start on the pitcher's motion and make the steal more easily than he could from first.

You must also keep the runner on third in his place by letting him know of your readiness to slam the ball down there if he gets too far off the bag. You make your throws to third on the inside of the bag, for the runner will be returning to the bag in fair territory. Come right out of your position to make this throw and let the ball go with full power.

Fielding Problems

The balls the catcher fields mostly are foul pop flies and bunts. The foul fly requires some getting used to, for you have to get your eye on it quickly or you may not be able to get under it in time. With long experience, many catchers can tell by the very sound the ball makes on the bat whether there will be a play on the foul and about where it is going. Until you develop this sixth sense, however, the thing you must do is get your mask off quickly and get your eye on the ball. You sweep off your mask with one fast upward move of your right hand. But *hold on* to the mask until you have spotted the ball. Once you know where the ball is, give the mask a good toss well away in the opposite direction and hustle after the ball. If it is straight up over your head, position yourself so the ball seems to be coming down on your nose. Then catch the ball with the glove flat, about eye level, and make your catch high. Making it high will enable you to get another grab at it in case the ball pops out. If the ball is coming down behind you or off to one side, let it lead you a little. The ball has a tendency to spin back toward you and it is easier to reach for it than to back-pedal after it. Sometimes, if there are high stands, there is a movement of air back toward the

Once you spot the ball, get rid of your mask.

diamond that will exaggerate the natural spin of the
ball. And remember, these balls have lots of spin, so
they will hop right out of the glove unless they are
quickly smothered with the bare hand.

Catch the ball high. If it bounces out of your glove you may have another chance at it before it hits the ground.

Anything coming down behind the plate is yours, of course. You must also try for any foul pops along the baselines that are within reasonable range. The first baseman or the third baseman may be after these also

and the pitcher will decide who has the better chance—
you or the fielder. If the pitcher calls you off, lay off at
once. Do not risk clobbering your teammate by per-
sisting in trying for a ball that he is going for. But if the
pitcher does not call you off, get to the ball just as fast
as you can scramble.

If you can catch a foul pop with men on base, never
forget that they can advance after the catch at their
own risk, so once you have the ball tight in your hand,
look quickly to see if the runner is going. Sometimes, if
you have to go all the way to the backstop after the foul,
you may be a long long way from second. The pitcher is
likely to be near the plate when you catch the ball with
a man on third, so you must look for a relay man at the
pitcher's mound. If there is no man there to take a
throw, hang on to the ball, even if the runner on first is
going down to second. But if the relay man is there—
and you should school your shortstop to get there on
such a play—you can hammer the ball to him and he
can either snap to second or fire it right back to the
plate, depending on whether the runner on third tries
for home or not.

Bunts are much more of a problem than foul pops
and they need a lot more practice. Do not stint on the
practice you may get scrambling out for a ball that is
rolling on the ground in front of you. You have to work
until it becomes instinctive with you to trail these balls
to the *left* (except when they go right up the third-base
line) and to keep your eye on the ball until it is safely
in your hand. No matter how urgent the situation, never
try to grab up the ball while watching the runner. Keep
your eye on the ball and go after it with *both hands*.
You may round it up with the glove and grab it with the
throwing hand. Then straighten up and gun the ball
overhand to the base. Sidearm and underhand throws

82

Keep your eye on the ball until it is safely in your hand.

should be avoided unless the situation is desperate. They have a tendency to curve and dip, and are much harder for the baseman to handle. Also they do not have the speed of the overhand throw. Throw hard in your natural motion, with your eye on the target. But always be sure there is a target. No matter how many voices are telling you which base to throw to, you look at the base and be sure there is someone covering it.

A throw to first should go down inside the baseline. The throw to second should go straight to the bag. But you will not often have a chance to nail the runner at second on a sacrifice bunt unless you get hold of the ball instantly. When you do succeed in pouncing on the ball before it has a chance to roll away, look at once to see if you can get the lead runner, either at second or third. You must decide in a split second if you have a chance and then let the ball go full steam without any hesitation. If there is no chance you must get off your throw to first instantly.

When you throw to third base on a force, you throw the ball about shoulder high, inside the baseline. If it is a tag play you have to get the ball down low, on the inside of the bag, where the baseman can make the tag without having to reach.

Trailing the bunt to the left means staying to one side of the ball, with your throwing hand closest to it. It is impossible to field a bunt and get off a quick throw if you field it directly in front of your body. If you stay to the left of the ball, you will come up facing the target and ready to throw. But if the ball goes down the third baseline, you will find it handier to keep to the *right* of the ball. Otherwise, when you field it, you have to take an awkward backward step to be in position to throw. If you are on the right of this ball, you can allow your natural momentum to take you right around in a complete turn to face first base and get off a hard throw.

You have to *catch* throws or putouts as well as make them. Some players shy away from the catcher's job because they exaggerate the danger of getting hurt through colliding with a runner at the plate. Actually there are not many collisions of that sort in a game and usually you can make your putout without too much bodily contact. Your job after all is not to rack the runner up but just to put him out and you can do that by just putting the ball on him.

There are times naturally when you have to get down and block off the plate (you cannot do this unless you have the ball) but even then you do not have to inter-

84

pose your whole body between runner and plate. And if you stay alert and hold your ground, there is not much danger he will hurt you. The runner wants to score and there is no advantage to him in piling into you. If he can see a piece of the plate, he is going to go for that.

If the throw to the plate comes from the right field side of the diamond, the way to receive it is with your left foot blocking off the plate. If it comes from the other side, your right foot can close off the plate. This kind of positioning will prompt the runner to use a hook slide toward the open corner of the plate and you will be able to put the tag on him without a collision. If the runner slides, he is going to run into your foot and your shinguard will protect you. Provided the ball is accurate and on time, you can drop right down and set the ball (held solidly in *both* hands) right where he must slide into it. Whether he uses the hook slide or slides straight in, he is going to have a hard time getting around that planted foot to avoid the tag.

Some strong catchers, however, prefer to await the throw by straddling the rear of the plate, then dropping down on one or both knees to block off the plate completely as soon as they have the ball.

If the throw has the runner beaten by a good margin and it comes in on target, you can take the throw close to the plate and move up to meet the runner. The sooner you can put the tag on him the less chance he has of scoring. You must hold the ball *tightly* in your hand. You do not need to crash into the runner or try to keep him from getting by. Approach him from *outside* the baseline, put the tag on him and get out of there. You can slow him down with your glove hand if you want to. But don't try to be nonchalant and keep the ball in your glove. Hold it tight in your fingers, as you tag him.

If the throw is well off the plate, do not stand too long at the plate waiting for it. Get out and meet the ball. If you don't get hold of it you can do nothing. And don't waste time watching the runner. Keep your eye fixed on the ball until you have hold of it. *Then* turn to deal with the runner.

You may even have to dive at the runner to put the tag on him. But if you do that, make sure you have a secure grip on the ball. Hold the ball in the bare hand, and put the glove over it to make sure it does not get jarred loose. Remember, you are not trying to stop the runner, just tag him and put him out. He can run all the way to the backstop then, if he wants to. He'll still be out.

If the play is close, you may have to go to your knees in the runner's path to make sure you get the ball down before he reaches the plate. But whatever you do, always make sure you have a safe grip on the ball. The safest grip is to hold it in two hands, fingers clutching it and glove guarding it. Many a runner will come right into you in hopes of jarring the ball loose. Let them come. Tag them and then jump clear. And don't hesitate to shove the batter aside if he gets in your way. You cannot interfere with the batter as a pitch comes in, but once you have the ball in your hands, the ground belongs to you.

Sometimes you can pick a man off third with a convincing bluff throw. That is, you pretend to fire the ball down to second but hold on to it and immediately check the runner on third. If he has broken from the base, a quick throw will hang him up on the baseline. Of course this usually means that you lose the runner at second but that is what you want to do—trade off a runner at third for a runner at second and an extra out. Your bluff, however, has got to be a convincing one. You cannot

If the play is close at the plate, you may have to go down on one or both knees.

fool the runner with a half-hearted imitation of a throw. You must bang the ball hard with a full motion of the arm and a stride toward the base—but hold tight to the ball as you do it. In other words, you must make all the motions exactly as if you were really throwing the ball.

The runner on this play has got to start as soon as you make the throw if he is to make it safely home, so if your moves are convincing enough you can do the opposition a lot of damage by taking that potential run off third. Sometimes, instead of a bluff throw on this play, a club will use a cut-off throw. That is, you will throw the ball hard, as if to the second baseman, but instead you will fire it right to the pitcher, or to the shortstop cutting in directly behind the mound. Then the ball will be returned instantly to you and you will either put the tag on the runner from third or catch him in a rundown.

Every time a batter swings at a pitch and misses it with men on base, you should check the runner to see if you can pick him off. If you have quicker reflexes than he does, you may be able to get a throw off before he recovers from the start he has taken toward the next base. And when a batter misses a bunt attempt, as even big-league batters sometimes do, the runner is likely to be left leaning hard the wrong way—an easy victim to a fast pick-off throw. Be alert for such opportunities to help your club all the time. Wiping the runner off the baselines is the best way in the world to help your pitcher, to lighten his burden, bring the smile back to his face, and move him closer to another win.

Game Strategy

A good catcher has to keep looking for different ways to beat the opposition. He has to remember that the batter and the baserunners are thinking right along with him and so he must try to stay a jump ahead. Of course the pitcher is thinking, too, and it requires teamwork to make sure your thinking is co-ordinated. Whatever you do, don't let your pitcher take matters too easy on the weak end of the batting order. There are pitchers who cannot help easing up a little when they get down to number seven and number eight in the order, or who keep looking past them to the next inning. The weak hitters are only comparatively weak. They have low averages because they cannot hit hard against good pitching. But off-speed stuff and curves that hang may be exactly the sort of pitching they can do well with, and if you let your pitcher ease up on them, they may tee off.

Remind your pitcher (and yourself), therefore, that

the weak end of the batting order is what he is going to grow fat on and he should bear down on them to get his strike-outs and pop-ups.

Against tough opposition, too, there is sometimes danger of a pitcher's "over-concentrating." That is an odd term to use because one of the secrets of good pitching is concentration. But a pitcher over-concentrates when he begins to put more stress on his thinking than on his pitching. He starts to fret about pitching to spots and worry over his choice of pitches, instead of rearing back to throw strikes. When a pitcher has good stuff, he does not need to fret too much about working the edges of the strike zone. If he throws strikes, and his pitches are alive, they are going to cut the corners of the plate anyway. Over-concentration, if that is the right word for it, usually results in taking a little off the best pitches for the sake of imaginary "accuracy" and "control." Encourage your pitcher, even as he is bearing down and centering his whole mind on the job, to have confidence in his stuff and to throw strikes, to challenge the hitters without any doubt about whether his pitches are going to move properly. If he begins to substitute nagging doubt and second-guessing for his natural instincts, he will actually lose some of his effectiveness. You have to help by keeping his confidence high, even when he is getting hit, and by urging him to let you do the thinking.

If you can get through the first five innings of a game without running into trouble, you are usually in very good shape, as far as pitching goes. After that, you can urge your pitcher to throw *low* strikes the rest of the way. Perhaps you have been able to conserve his best pitch through the first innings, to use toward the end of the game, when the opposition will be changing their tactics to try to push runs across. If you can do that—

and you can do it only if you manage to stay out of tight spots in the first five innings—you can stay in command, because you will be able to wheel in your secret weapon—the get-out pitch—when the enemy starts to bring in the pinch-hitters and begins to scheme to get men on the bases.

For a catcher, to nail a baserunner with a pitch-out is like a heavy hitter's belting a ball over the fence, or a pitcher's striking out the side. It is one of the best feelings you can find in baseball. But you have to use your head in calling for this pitch. It gives a ball to the batter and may put the pitcher behind in the count. So you call for it only when you *must* learn if there is a play on or when you are certain the hit-and-run or the steal is on. Not all coaches and ballplayers are careful about concealing signs and sometimes you can get a tip-off from the movements the batter makes. Or you may just figure from the strategic situation and the ability of the runner on first that the man will be going. If you figure things right, you get a good outside high pitch that you can fire right down to second and catch the runner by half a block. It is a thrill you will never forget.

When you have the pitcher at bat with a man on first, or when a batter who is known as a clever bunter comes up in the same circumstances, particularly in the late innings, you will want to find out if there is a play in the works. A pitchout will reveal whether the batter is planning to bunt. (Once in a while it may even find the runner leaning a little too much toward second in hopes of getting an extra good start, and you will be able to pick him off.) Occasionally, when you see the bunt has been called, you can do yourself some good (provided the pitcher has good control) by immediately calling for another pitchout. But usually what you try to do is not to keep the man from bunting but give him a pitch that he will find difficult to bunt safely. A good high pitch may cause the batter to pop up, and may even present you with a quick double play if the runner has foolishly started before making sure the ball is on the ground.

But the pitchout has got to be really *out*—too far away from the plate for the batter to reach with his bat, and high enough for you to get off a quick throw. Don't anticipate it too much, or its value will be lost. Stay right in the slot, in your regular stance, until the ball is on its way.

Late in a tie game with a runner on third base and less than two out, you can look for a squeeze play. You do not too often see the suicide squeeze, in which the runner starts with the pitch and the batter *must* get his bat on the ball. Most managers use the safety squeeze, with the runner going full tilt only when the ball is on the ground.

When you suspect a squeeze is on, or when the pitcher, as he starts to release the ball, sees that the runner is on his way, the ball should come in high and tight to a right-handed batter. Indeed it is usually recommended that the pitcher throw right at the batter, making it almost impossible to bunt and forcing him to bail out so you can lay the ball on the runner quickly. (Of course if the bases are full you cannot throw at the batter because if the pitch hits him a run is forced in anyway.)

If the batter is a left-hander, the pitch on a suspected squeeze play must be high and outside—a regular pitch-out that you can grab without any interference from the bat. (If the batter steps across the plate to hit it, he will be called out and if he gets in your way the runner will be out.) In either case the run cannot score.

Do not make the mistake of pitching around a batter just because he is going to bunt. Let him bunt. But make him bunt a high pitch.

But if the batter is trying to hit behind the runner, on a hit-and-run play or to move a runner over from second to third, he will be hoping for a fairly high pitch, which he can place more easily. So you pitch low to *him*. And if he is a right-hander you keep the ball inside.

You should always make sure your pitcher cooperates with the fielders in the placement of his pitches. If there is a run in scoring position and the infield is pulled in to cut off the runner at the plate, you must make sure the ball comes in low every time. What you do not want is a ball the batter can dump over the heads of the infielders. A low pitch is more likely to result in a ground ball. Of course a sinker-ball specialist has just the medicine for a situation like this. But a good low fast ball is not easy to get into the air either.

Likewise if you are trying to keep a man from hitting behind the runner, you make sure your pitcher keeps the ball outside to a left-hander and inside to a right-hander. And you keep the ball away from a man who is trying to pull it into the seats. Of course you cannot always do exactly what you want with every pitcher. If your man's best pitch is a fast ball that tails in to a left-hander, you cannot discard it for the sake of strategy. You occasionally have to compromise and use your judgment on where the percentages lie.

In a tight ball game it is often best strategy to pitch around the big hitter when there are men on base. This does not mean walking him—although if you have first base open that is sometimes good tactics. It means keeping the ball away from his strength, putting into the strike zone only the sort of pitches he cannot handle effectively, wasting the weak pitches, risking a base on balls rather than feeding him a pitch he can drive out of the park. It is good practice, too, when you are in a tight game, to take extra care not to put a man on base before the big man comes up.

If you are not sure of the big hitter's weakness, the safest pitch to use is your pitcher's best, thrown low and to the outside edge of the strike zone. The heavy hitters usually like inside pitches that they can pull for distance, so you try to give them what they *don't* like. But remember there *are* some heavy hitters who like low pitches and have learned to drive them a long way.

Of course one of the best things that can happen to a pitcher who has put a man on base is a double play. Very few things will cheer a pitcher more than to get two outs on one batted ball. Naturally it takes good infielders to create such a play. But the pitcher and catcher must play their parts too. That is, they must work to get the batter to hit the ball on the ground and to hit it where the fielders can reach it. When a batter is trying to hit behind a runner he is more concerned with bat control than with distance and he needs to be handled with more care. Outside pitches keep a left-hander from hitting too easily to the right of the diamond, and inside pitches do the same thing for a right-handed batter. Low pitches tend to keep the ball on the ground. But breaking pitches, or any off-speed pitches, are somewhat easier to deal with when a man has choked up on his bat and is trying to place the ball. So sliders and fast balls, thrown low in the strike zone, are often the surest ingredients to use to make a double play.

It is good to bear in mind that a fast pitch is what is needed in almost any situation that may require the batter to hit behind the runner—or on a squeeze play. It is also the recommended prescription when a sacrifice is expected or when the infield is playing in tight to cut off a run—or for that matter, when a hit-and-run possibility exists. That is simply because a fast ball (high and inside to protect against a squeeze bunt or a hit behind the runner from a right-handed batter) is harder for a batter to "place."

Some Points to Remember

Remember that when you have a force-out at home you also have a force-out at first base and at every other base. First base offers you the best chance for an extra out because the runner from the plate does not start with a lead. You will want to receive the throw, therefore, in a position to get off a fast throw to first if at all possible. Naturally you must make the put put at home first, but even if you miss that, you may still have a chance to get the man at first.

On a force-out at the plate, catchers usually await the throw behind the plate, or off on the first base side, in foul territory. This is to give the fielder a target that will not cause him to hit the runner. But you can get a better and faster throw off to first if you await the throw with your right foot on the plate. This enables you to step directly toward first to fire the ball down there as soon as you get hold of it. There is danger on this play that the runner may slide into your planted foot or may run across in front of you, so you need to be strong and agile.

On any play at or near the plate—a foul fly, a throw home, a bunt you must field—you should get your mask off, unless the play is so close you simply don't have time, as on a steal of home. You can sweep your mask off in a split second with your right hand and take care to toss it into foul territory (*away* from the ball in case of a pop foul). And when you hustle down to back up first base on a bases-empty situation you do not need to take your mask with you. But remember: toss it into *foul* territory.

To get off a good throw, you have to start with your weight on your *right* foot. You make a natural shift of your weight to the right foot when you shift to the first base side of the plate to receive a pitch. But when you have to take a pitch on the third base of the plate, you will find yourself with the weight on your left foot. Your best move then is a kind of hopping turn, to swing your weight to the right foot and your body back to the plate.

Another good point to remember is that on foul pop flies, the ball spins *toward* the playing field. Be ready for this as you wait for a high pop near the plate. And bear in mind that it is easier to reach out for a ball in front of you than to back-pedal for one behind you.

It is up to you, because you have the whole play in your vision, to tell the cut-off man whether to cut off a throw from the outfield or let it go through. Don't be afraid to make yourself heard on the diamond. You are in the best position to captain much of the defense. Yell out your instructions at the top of your voice: "Cut it off!" or "Let it go!" Don't let anyone tell you later that he didn't hear you.

In general, the time to call for breaking pitches and change-of-pace is when the batter is ahead of the pitcher —that is, when he will be looking for "his" pitch and is ready to tee off on it.

Don't forget to let your infielders know when you are going to call for a pitch-out, or you may find the base has not been covered. Give the pick-off sign to the in-fielder *first*. Make sure he acknowledges it by some agreed signal, such as glove on knee, bare hand to cap or other natural gesture. Then give the pitch-out sign to the pitcher.

You can give your sign to the pitcher well back from

the plate, then step forward to be as close as possible to the batter. There is less chance of getting hurt if you are close to the bat.

Do not be careless about protecting your bare hand as you await the pitch. Keep it folded and get it *behind* the glove as the ball comes in.

Take good care of all your equipment, especially gloves and shoes. Always have two pairs of shoes and two gloves—for breaking in and for game use.

All your throws should be overhand, except when you barely have time to beat the runner on a fielded bunt. An overhand throw will make up in speed what you may lose by straightening up to throw. Also you will be more accurate with your overhand throws.

Pace your pitcher if he gets impatient. You can do this most easily by simply holding on to the ball a little longer. But never lob a ball back with men on base. Get it into the pitcher's hands quickly.

Get after a bunt with top speed. You can sweep off the mask as you move out over the plate and a quick hop can put you into position to throw after you have fielded the bunt. Weight must be on your right foot to get off a good throw.

Don't ever stand in front of a runner to tag him out. At the plate, get down and put the ball where he must slide into it. On a play that is not close, move up to put the tag on. Approach the runner from outside the foul line, tag him, and get out of the way.

Never make a blind throw. Always look to make sure there is a fielder to throw to.

Keep up your spirits! Talk it up to your infield and to your pitcher! Don't let your infielders get out of position or start playing on their heels. Be alert, aggressive, and determined to win!

96